# JETS

# JETS

**Michael Sharpe**

Published by TAJ Books International LLC 2013

219 Great Lake Drive,

Cary, North Carolina, USA

27519

www.tajbooks.com

All notations of errors or omissions (author inquiries, permissions) concerning the content of this book should be addressed to

info@tajbooks.com.

ISBN 978-1-84406-315-4

Printed in China.

1 2 3 4 5 17 16 15 14 13

# CONTENTS

# INTRODUCTION

A jet aircraft is an aircraft propelled by jet engines. Jet aircraft generally fly much faster than propeller-powered aircraft and at higher altitudes—as high as 10,000 to 15,000 meters (about 33,000 to 49,000 feet). At these altitudes, jet engines achieve maximum efficiency over long distances. The engines in propeller-powered aircraft achieve their maximum efficiency at much lower altitudes. Jet aircraft can move faster than sound.

Henri Coand, a Romanian engineer, was the first to build a jet plane in 1910—the Coanda-1910. Later, two engineers, Frank Whittle in the United Kingdom and Hans von Ohain in Germany, developed the concept independently during the late 1930s, although credit for the first turbojet is given to Whittle. The concept had already been discussed as early as August 1928 by Frank Whittle at Flying School, Wittering, but Hans von Ohain also wrote in February 1936 to Ernst Heinkel, telling him of the design and its possibilities. It can be argued, however that A.A. Griffith, who published a paper in July 1926 on compressors and turbines, which he had been studying at the Royal Aircraft Establishment (RAE), also deserves credit, perhaps more than either Frank Whittle or Hans von Ohain.

The first turbine-equipped jet plane was designed on paper in late 1929 when Frank Whittle of the British Royal Air Force sent his concept to the Air Ministry to see if it would be of any interest to them. The first manufactured turbine jet plane was the Heinkel He 178 turbojet prototype of the German Air Force (Luftwaffe), piloted by Erich Warsitz on August 27, 1939.

The first flight of the Italian Caproni Campini N.1 motorjet prototype was on August 27, 1940. Test pilot Major Mario De Bernardi of the Regia Aeronautica was at the controls.

The British flew their Gloster E.28/39 prototype on May 15, 1941, powered by Sir Frank Whittle's turbojet, and piloted by Flt. Lt. P.G. Sayer. When the United States learned of the British work, it produced the Bell XP-59 with a version of the Whittle engine built by General Electric,

*The Heinkel He 178, the world's first aircraft to fly purely on turbojet power*

*A memorial to Sir Frank Whittle on the northern boundary of Farnborough Aerodrome in the U.K. with a full-scale model of the Gloster E28/39*

*The Italian Caproni Campini N.1 (CC.2)*

Bell X-1 became the first airplane to fly faster than the speed of sound. Piloted by U.S. Air Force Capt. Charles E. "Chuck" Yeager, the X-1 reached a speed of 1,127 kilometers (700 miles) per hour, Mach 1.06, at an altitude of 13,000 meters (43,000 feet).

In the 1940s, more reach is given to the long striking arm of the U.S. Air Force North American B-45C Tornado four-jet bomber, a "wing tip tank" version of the B-45. The tanks pack much more range into the Tornado's normal tactical radius of over 800 miles. Black paint on the inside of the tanks and engine nacelles reduce glare. The sleek bombers carry a payload of over 10 tons and are in the 550 miles per hour speed class. (U.S. Air Force photo)

*Gloster E.28/39 prototype*

*Nakajima J9Y Kikka*

and flew it on September 12, 1942, piloted by Col. Laurence Craigie.

The first operational jet fighter was the Messerschmitt Me 262, made by Germany during late World War II. It was the fastest conventional aircraft of World War II, although the rocket-powered Messerschmitt Me 163 Komet was faster.

Mass production started in 1944, too late for a decisive effect on the outcome of the war. About the same time, the United Kingdom's Gloster Meteor was limited to defense of the U.K. against the V1 flying bomb and ground-attack operations over Europe in the last months of the war. The Imperial Japanese Navy also developed jet aircraft in 1945,

*The Bell XP-59 flies a test mission. The aircraft was America's first jet-powered aircraft and made its maiden flight on October 1, 1942.*

*The first operational jet fighter was the Messerschmitt Me 262.*

*P-59 Airacomet*

Col. Benjamin O. Davis, Jr., commander of the 51st Fighter Interceptor Wing, leads a three-ship F-86F Sabre formation during the Korean War in 1954. Col. Davis, a Tuskegee Airman, was one of the first African-American wing commanders.

In the 1950s, the Convair YB-60 swept-wing, eight-jet bomber is shown here in the first flight view of the U.S. Air Force's latest addition to its air arsenal. Equipped with eight Pratt & Whitney turbojet engines, the most powerful of their type then in use, the YB-60 was rolled out of the factory at Consolidated Vultee Aircraft Corporation's Fort Worth, Texas, Division on April 6, 1952, for engine run-ups and ground tests. The first flight, on April 18, 1952, occurred just 14 days after installation of its final engine. The plane's needle-nose appearance originates from a slender boom used for test purposes.

*BOAC Havilland Comet jetliner, the first commercial jet service*

including the Nakajima J9Y Kikka, a crude copy of the Me-262

On November 8, 1950, during the Korean War, U.S. Air Force Lt. Russell J. Brown, flying in an F-80, intercepted two North Korean MiG-15s near the Yalu River and shot them down in the first jet-to-jet dogfight in history.

The first commercial jet service was operated by BOAC from London to Johannesburg, South Africa, in 1952 with the de Havilland Comet jetliner.

The fastest military jet plane was the SR-71 Blackbird at

*The fastest military jet plane was the SR-71 Blackbird at Mach 3.2*

*The fastest commercial jet plane was the Tupolev Tu-144 at Mach 2.35.*

Mach 3.2. The fastest commercial jet plane was the Tupolev Tu-144 at Mach 2.35.

Modern airliners cruise at speeds of 0.75 to 0.85 Mach, or 75% to 85% of the speed of sound (420 to 580 mph/ 680-900 km/h). The speed of sound predominantly depends on air temperature (hardly at all on pressure), so the Mach number for the speed of a jet also varies with atmospheric conditions. NASA and the U.S. Federal Aviation Administration have been promoting very light jets (VLJ), which are small general aviation aircraft seating 4 to 8

*The Cessna Citation Mustang, an example of the VLJ (Very Light Jet)*

The Ling-Temco-Vought A-7 Corsair II is a carrier-capable subsonic light attack aircraft introduced to replace the Douglas A-4 Skyhawk. It was introduced in 1967 and retired in 1991.

The Vickers Nene Viking G-AJPH was later converted back to a standard Viking. This was the very first civilian jet aircraft, first flight tested by the Great Joseph "Mutt" Summers.

Tupolev Tu-104A OK-LDA CSA Czech Ailines

passengers.

A jet airliner is a passenger airplane that is powered by jet engines. This term is sometimes contracted to jetliner. In contrast to today's relatively fuel-efficient, turbofan-powered air travel, first-generation jet airliner travel was noisy and fuel was inefficient. These inefficiencies were addressed by the invention of turboprop and turbofan engines. The first airliners with turbojet propulsion were experimental conversions of the Avro Lancastrian piston-engined airliner, which were flown with several types of early jet engine,

including the de Havilland Ghost and the Rolls-Royce Nene. These aircraft retained the two inboard piston engines, the jets being housed in the outboard nacelles and were therefore of "mixed" propulsion.

The first airliner with full jet power was the Nene-powered Vickers VC.1 Viking G-AJPH, which first flew on the April 6, 1948. The first purpose-built jet airliner was the de Havilland Comet, which first flew in 1949 and entered service in 1952. Also developed in 1949 was the Avro Jetliner, and although it never reached production, the

Corse Air International Sud Aviation Caravelle at the Basel, Switzerland, airport in October 1985

*1978 Pan Am Clipper "Mount Vernon" Boeing 707*

*Pan American World Airways Douglas DC-8-33 N805PA at Stockholm-Arlanda Airport in July 1965*

term jetliner caught on as a generic term for all passenger jet aircraft.

These first jet airliners were followed some years later by the Sud Aviation Caravelle, Tupolev Tu-104 (second in service), Boeing 707, Douglas DC-8, and Convair 880. National prestige was attached to developing prototypes and bringing these first-generation designs into service. There was also a strong nationalism in purchasing policy, such that the Boeing and Douglas products became closely associated with Pan Am, while BOAC ordered British-made Comets.

These two airlines with strong nautical traditions of command hierarchy rank and chain of command, retained from their days of operations with flying boats, undoubtably were quick to capitalize upon, with the help of advertising agencies, the linking of the "speed of jets" with the safe and secure "luxury of ocean liners" among public perception.

Aeroflot used Russian Tupolevs, while Air France

*American Airlines BAC One-Elevan*

introduced French Caravelles. Commercial realities dictated exceptions, however, as few airlines could risk missing out on a superior product: American airlines ordered the pioneering Comet (but later canceled when the Comet ran into fatigue problems); Canadian, British, and European airlines could not ignore the better operating economics of the Boeing 707 and the DC-8; whereas some American airlines ordered the

*Boeing B-52D-70-BO (SN 56-0582) is refueled by Boeing KC-135A-BN (SN 55-3127).*

*Continental Douglas DC-9 twin jet*

Caravelle.

Boeing became the most successful of the early manufacturers. The KC-135 Stratotanker and military versions of the 707 remain operational, mostly as tankers or freighters. The basic configuration of the Boeing, Convair, and Douglas aircraft jet airliner designs, with widely spaced podded engines underslung on pylons beneath a swept wing, proved to be the most common arrangement and was most easily compatible with the large-diameter high-bypass turbofan engines that subsequently prevailed for reasons of quietness and fuel efficiency.

The de Havilland and Tupolev designs had engines incorporated within the wings next to the fuselage, a concept that endured only within military designs, while the Caravelle-pioneered engines were mounted either side of the rear fuselage. In the 1960s, when jet airliners were powered by slim, low-bypass engines, many aircraft used the rear-engined, T-tail configuration, such as the BAC One-Eleven, Douglas DC-9 twin jets; Boeing 727, Hawker Siddeley Trident, Tupolev Tu-154 trijets; and the paired multi-engined Ilyushin Il-62 and Vickers VC-10, whose engines were mounted upon the aft fuselage. This engine arrangement survives into the 21st century on numerous twin-engined Douglas DC-9 derivatives plus newer short

*Champion Air Boeing 727-2S7/Adv aircraft (N686CA) at Los Angeles International Airport (LAX/KLAX)*

*Pan Am Boeing 747 at the Zurich airport in May 1985*

haul and range turbofan powered regional aircraft, such as the "regional jet airliners" built by Bombardier, Embraer, and until recently, Fokker. Other "jetliner" developments, however, such as the concept of rocket-assisted take-offs (RATO) and water-injection as used and tested on first-generation passenger jets as well as trailing edge-mounted powerplants, or afterburners, also known as reheat that were used on supersonic jetliners (SST), such as the Concorde and Tupolev Tu-144, have been relegated to the past.

For business jets, the rear-engined universal configuration pioneered by the turbojet-powered early Learjet 23, North American Sabreliner, and Lockheed JetStar is common practice on smaller bizjet aircraft because the wing is too close to the ground to accommodate underslung engines.

This differs from the early-generation jet airliners, whose design engineers slung jet engines on the rear to increase wing lift performance and at the same time reduce cabin noise of the lower bypass "turbojet" engines.

Airliner descriptions are commonly broken down into the distinctions of the generally long-haul civilian passenger

*Mauritania government G-1159 Gulfstream II at the Basel, Switzerland, airport in March 1987*

*Eclipse 500*

jumbo and widebody jet airliners and of the short-haul civilian passenger "jet" airliners. Among some of these categories included among the short-haul civilian passenger "jets" are both longer- and shorter-ranged "narrow-body jet and regional jet types." The terms "civilian," "turbine-powered," "jet," "passenger," "air," and "liner" are routinely dropped from descriptions of "jet aircraft," which can lead to confusion among those practicing language purity.

Almost all production business jets, such as General Dynamics' Gulfstream and the Gates Lear Jet (now built by Bombardier), have had two or three engines, although the Jetstar, an early business jet, had four. Advances in engine reliability and power have rendered four-engine designs obsolete and only Dassault Aviation still builds three-engine

models (in the Falcon line). The emerging market for so-called very light jets and personal jets has introduced (at least on paper) several single-engine designs as well.

Almost all business jets have rear-mounted engines because the wing (mounted low for performance reasons) is

*The Maverick SmartJET costs approximately $899,000.*

25

*A B-52 Stratofortress leads a formation of two F-16 Fighting Falcons, two Japan Air Self-Defense Force F-2 attack fighters, and two U.S. Navy EA-6B Prowlers on February 15, 2010, near Guam during Exercise Cope North.*

*An early-production Boeing 737-100 at Manchester airport in the U.K. in 1972; Lufthansa was the launch customer for the Boeing 737, the most successful passenger jet ever.*

too near the ground for engines to be slung underneath it.

Airliners are sometimes converted into luxury business jets. Such converted aircraft are often used by celebrities with a large entourage or press corps, or by sports teams. Such airliners often face operational restrictions based on runway length or local noise restrictions.

A focus of development is at the low end of the market with small models, many far cheaper than existing business jets. Many of these fall into the VLJ category and are used by the air taxi industry. Cessna has developed the Mustang, a six-place twinjet (2 crew + 4 passengers) available for $2.55 million. A number of smaller manufacturers have planned even cheaper jets; the first is the Eclipse 500 which has become available at around $1.5 million. It remains to be seen whether the new jet manufacturers will complete their designs or find the market required to sell their jets at the low prices planned.

There are approximately 11,000 business jets in the

*Air France was the launch customer for the Airbus A320, Airbus' most successful aircraft; sales of 5,432 as of January 2013.*

*X-43 Scramjet*

worldwide fleet with the vast majority of them based in the United States or owned by U.S. companies. The European market is the next largest, with growing activity in the Middle East, Asia, and Central America. Because new aircraft orders can take two to three years for delivery, there is a large pre-owned marketplace with immediate availability. Since 1996, the term "fractional jet" has been used in connection with business aircraft owned by a consortium of companies. Costly overheads such as flight crew, hangarage,

and maintenance can be shared through such arrangements. In addition to outright new or pre-owned acquisition by aircraft users, new business jets are often purchased using a system of ownership positions. Usually this entails a deposit that reserves a future delivery of the aircraft: a "position" of ownership for a future date, normally three to five years in in advance. Additional deposits are paid as the aircraft nears completion. The future positions can be bought and sold by the owners, with any remaining balances due to the

*Thirteen different flights by eight pilots flying the X-15 met the USAF spaceflight criterion by exceeding the altitude of 50 miles (80 km), thus qualifying the pilots for astronaut status.*

*Air Force Global Strike Command officials assumed responsibility for the Air Force's nuclear-capable bomber force, including the B-52 Stratofortress and B-2 Spirit shown here on February 1, 2010.*

manufacturer. There is an active market in aircraft positions, and during turbulent economic times these positions are sometimes abandoned, leaving the manufacturer with the deposit funds, as well as the need to sell the aircraft position to another buyer.

Most people use the term "jet aircraft" to denote gas-turbine-based airbreathing jet engines, but rockets and scramjets are both also propelled by them. The fastest airbreathing jet aircraft is the unmanned X-43 scramjet at around Mach 9-10. The fastest manned (rocket) aircraft is the X-15 at Mach 6.85. The Space Shuttle, while far faster than the X-43 or X-15, is not regarded as a jet aircraft during ascent, nor during re-entry and landing because it is unpowered during this phase of operation.

The future of the aircraft industry is uncertain. Regional jets of less than 100 seats are forecast to disappear completely from commercial airline fleets, and with both Boeing and Airbus experiencing problems with their newest models

the 787 and A380, respectively, future development will slow greatly until current issues can be resolved. Military spending on aircraft worldwide is slowing dramatically as governments face budget constraints following the effects of the financial crisis of 2008. China may well emerge in the coming decades as the only growth manufatcurer in both commercial and military aircraft. Airbus has a joint venture in Tianjin producing four A320s a month. As China uses its vast trade surplus to invest in aerospace, it's only a matter of time before China will be competing head on with the likes of Boeing and Airbus in the commercial field and the defense companies of the west for military aircraft.

The aircraft featured on the following pages—in chronological order—are some of the greatest jets ever developed for commercial, private, and military fleets.

*Airbus A380 suffered from wing cracks and engine problems.*

Boeing's latest plane, the B787, has suffered from battery problems as well as a fuel leak that caused the above ANA plane to make an emergency landing. State-of-the-art technology will track every one of the new planes, sending information directly to Boeing for analysis.

# P-80 SHOOTING STAR

The Lockheed P-80 Shooting Star was developed relatively late in the war. Its design was notable because it was the first jet fighter to enter service for the United States. After an Allied discovery of the German Me262 jets in 1943, Lockheed was pushed to develop a comparable machine as quickly as possible. The whole process from design to production was completed in an astonishingly short 143 days. The first Shooting Star XP-80 prototype—dubbed "Lulu-Belle"—took flight on January 8, 1944. The British-supplied H1-B engine and 2,200 lb thrust did not provide enough power for the aircraft, and a second prototype was produced. The XP-80A included the larger General Electric I-40 engine and almost double the amount of thrust compared to its predecessor. Test flights did not go well and the plane received negative reviews from pilots, claiming they were too big and too slow. A third prototype (YP-80A) was developed and was yet again dimensionally larger and much heavier than previous models. Its J33-GE-11 and the J33-A-9 engines were located in the fuselage. Testing the P-80 Shooting Stars proved to be very dangerous for pilots; Lockheed head test pilot Milo Burcham lost his life flying the third prototype, while Tony LeVier narrowly escaped death, breaking his back after bailing out of the second prototype nicknamed "Gray Ghost." American ace Richard Bong also lost his life on a later flight of the P-80 production planes when the main fuel pump failed. It was later discovered that Bong failed to use the emergency fuel pump that could have prevented the accident. With these final modifications, the first production order for the P-80A was placed on April 4, 1944. Despite rushing the order, the aircraft's service entry was in February 1945 and it did not see any combat in World War II. Many P-80A Shooting Stars were transferred to Naval service in June 1945.

# B-47 STRATOJET

The Boeing Model 450 B-47 Stratojet was a long-range, six-engine, jet-powered medium bomber built to fly at high subsonic speeds and at high altitudes. It was primarily designed to drop nuclear bombs on the Soviet Union. With its engines carried in pods under the swept wing, the B-47 was a major innovation in post-World War II combat jet design, and helped lead to modern jet airliners. The B-47 entered service with the U.S. Air Force's Strategic Air Command (SAC) in 1951. It never saw combat as a bomber, but was a mainstay of SAC's bomber strength during the 1950s and early 1960s, and remained in use as a bomber until 1965. By 1956, the U.S. Air Force had 28 wings of B-47 bombers and five wings of RB-47 reconnaissance aircraft. The bombers were the first line of America's strategic nuclear deterrent, often operating from forward bases in the U.K., Morocco, Spain, Alaska, Greenland, and Guam. B-47 bombers were often set up on "one-third" alert, with a third of the operational aircraft available sitting on hardstands or an alert ramp adjacent to the runway, loaded with fuel and nuclear weapons, crews on standby, ready to attack the USSR at short notice. Crews were also trained to perform "minimum interval take-offs" (MITO), with one bomber following the other into the air at intervals of as little as 15 seconds, in order to launch all bombers as fast as possible. A MITO could be hazardous because the bombers left turbulence and the first-generation turbojet engines with water injection systems produced dense black smoke that blinded pilots in the following aircraft. The B-52 began to assume nuclear alert duties and the number of B-47 bomber wings started to be reduced. B-47 production ceased in 1957, al though modifications and rebuilds continued after that.

# MARTIN B-57 CANBERRA

The Martin B-57 Canberra is a twin-engine jet bomber and reconnaissance aircraft that entered service in the 1950s. At the outbreak of the Korean War in 1950, the U.S. Air Force found itself in dire need of an all-weather interdiction aircraft. The piston-engined Douglas A-26 Invaders were limited to daytime and fair weather operations and were in short supply. Thus, on September 16, 1950, the USAF issued a request for a jet-powered bomber with a top speed of 630 mph (1,020 km/h), ceiling of 40,000 feet (12,190 meters), and range of 1,150 miles (1,850 kilometers). A full all-weather capability and secondary reconnaissance role had to be in the design. The contenders included the Martin XB-51 and the North American B-45 Tornado and AJ Savage. In an extremely rare move, foreign aircraft, including the Canadian Avro CF-100 Canuck and the British English Electric Canberra, were also given consideration. The AJ and B-45 were quickly dismissed because their outdated designs had limited potential. The CF-100 was too small and lacked the sufficient range. On February 21, 1951, a British Canberra B.2 became the first-ever jet to make a nonstop unrefueled flight across the Atlantic Ocean, arriving in the United States for USAF evaluation. On April 3, 1951, Martin was granted the license to build Canberras, designated B-57 (Martin Model 272) in the U.S. Remarkably, this was the first foreign aircraft purchased by the USAF since the British Airco DH.4 of World War I. The first B-57A were largely identical to the Canberra B.2 with the exception of more powerful Armstrong-Siddeley Sapphire engines of 7,200 lbf (32 kN) of thrust, also license-built in the U.S. as Wright J65s. The first aircraft were accepted by the USAF on August 20, 1953. During the production run from 1953 to 1957, a total of 403 B-57s were built, two are still operational at NASA.

# B-52 STRATOFORTRESS

The Boeing B-52 Stratofortress is a long-range, eight-engine strategic bomber flown by the U.S. Air Force (USAF) since 1954, replacing the Convair B-36 and Boeing B-47. Although built for the role of Cold War–era nuclear deterrent, its conventional capabilities play the more important role in USAF operations today. Its long-range, heavy weapons load and comparatively economical operation (compared to the rest of the USAF strategic bomber fleet) are extremely useful. For more than 50 years, the B-52 Stratofortress has been the backbone of the manned strategic bomber force for the United States. The B-52 is capable of dropping or launching a wide array of weapons in the U.S. inventory, including free-fall (gravity bombs), cluster bombs, and precision-guided ordnance such as Joint Direct Attack Munitions. When updated with the latest technology, the B-52 will be capable of delivering the full complement of joint-developed weapons, allowing it to continue well into the 21st century as an important element of U.S. military capabilities. Current engineering analyses show the B-52's life span to extend beyond the year 2045. The B-52A first flew in August 1954 and the B model entered service in 1955. A total of 744 B-52s were built with the last, a B-52H, delivered in October 1962. Only the H model is still in the USAF inventory and is assigned to Air Combat Command and the Air Force Reserves. The oldest B-52 still flying was a B-52B that was built in 1955, although it also has the fewest flight hours of any surviving B-52. It was operated by NASA's Dryden Flight Research Center and was used for drop tests of various research aircraft until its retirement on December 17, 2004.

# AVRO VULCAN

The Avro Vulcan was a British delta-wing subsonic bomber, operated by the Royal Air Force from 1953 until 1984. The Vulcan was part of the RAF's V bomber force, which fulfilled the role of nuclear deterrent against the Soviet Union during the Cold War. Design work began at A.V. Roe in 1947 under Roy Chadwick. The Ministry of Defence specification required a bomber with a top speed of 500 knots (930 km/h), an operating ceiling of 50,000 feet (15,000 meters), a range of 3,000 nautical miles (5,500 kilometers) and a bomb load of 10,000 pounds (4,500 kilograms). Design work also began at Vickers and Handley Page. All three designs—Valiant, Victor, and Vulcan—were approved. The first full-scale prototype aircraft, the Type 698, made its maiden flight (after its designer had died) on August 31, 1952. The Vulcan name was not chosen until 1953. As part of Britain's independent nuclear deterrent, the Vulcan initially carried Britain's first nuclear weapon, the Blue Danube gravity bomb. The bomb load was gradually updated to Yellow Sun and then Red Beard, and after 1962, twenty-six Vulcan B.2As were armed with the Blue Steel missile. When Blue Steel was decommissioned and the replacement program for the Skybolt ALBM was canceled, the bombers reverted to gravity bomb loads despite the lack of credible deterrent value in this delivery method. Although the primary weapon for the Vulcan was nuclear, Vulcans could carry up to 21 x 1,000 lb (454 kg) bombs in a secondary role. The only combat missions involving the Vulcan took place in the 1982 Falklands War with Argentina, when a number of Vulcans flew the 3,380 nautical miles (6,300 kilometers) from Ascension Island to Stanley to bomb the occupied airfield there with conventional bombs in Operation Black Buck.

# U-2

The U-2, nicknamed Dragon Lady, is a single-seat, single-engine, high-altitude surveillance aircraft flown by the U.S. Air Force. It provides continuous day and night, high-altitude (70,000 feet, 21,000 meter-plus), all-weather surveillance of an area in direct support of U.S. and allied ground and air forces. It also provides critical intelligence to decision makers through all phases of conflict, including peacetime indications and warnings, crises, operations other than war, and major theater war. The aircraft are also used for electronic sensor research and development, satellite calibration, and satellite data validation. A classified budget document approved by the Pentagon on December 23, 2005, called for the termination of the U-2 program, with some planes being retired as early as 2007. But retirement of the U-2 has been delayed by gaps in capability if the fleet was removed from service. In 2009, the USAF stated that it planned to extend the U-2 retirement from 2012 until 2014 or later to allow more time to field Northrop Grumman's high-altitude, unmanned RQ-4 Global Hawk as a replacement. Beginning in 2010, the RQ-170 Sentinel began replacing U-2s operating from Osan Air Base, South Korea. The U-2 project was initiated in the early 1950s by the CIA which needed accurate information on the Soviet Union. Overflights of the Soviet Union with modified bombers started around 1951, but they were vulnerable to anti-aircraft fire and fighters, and a number of border flights were shot down. It was thought a high-altitude aircraft, such as the U-2, would be hard to detect and impossible to shoot down. Lockheed Corporation was given the assignment with an unlimited budget and a short time frame. Its Skunk Works performed remarkably, and the first flight occurred in August 1955. The U-2 made its first overflight of the Soviet Union in June 1956.

# KC-135 STRATOTANKER

The Boeing KC-135 Stratotanker is an aerial refueling tanker aircraft, first manufactured in 1956 and expected to remain in service into the 2040s. It is derived from the original Boeing jet transport proof-of-concept demonstrator, the Boeing 367-80 commonly called the Dash-80. As such, it has a narrower fuselage and is shorter than the Boeing 707 jetliner. Developed in the late 1950s, this basic airframe is characterized by swept wings and tail, four underwing mounted engine pods, a horizontal stabilizer mounted on the fuselage near the bottom of the vertical stabilizer with positive di-hedral on the two horizontal planes and a hi-frequency radio antenna, which protrudes forward from the top of the vertical fin or stabilizer. These basic features make it strongly resemble the commercial Boeing 707 and 720 aircraft although, under the skin, it's actually a different aircraft. Boeing's 367-80 was the basic design for the commercial Boeing 707 passenger aircraft as well as the KC-135A Stratotanker. In 1954 the USAF's Strategic Air Command ordered the first 29 of its future fleet of 732. The first aircraft flew in August 1956 and the initial production Stratotanker was delivered to Castle Air Force Base, California, in June 1957. The last KC-135 was delivered to the Air Force in 1965. In Southeast Asia, KC-135 Stratotankers made the air war different from all previous aerial conflicts. Midair refueling brought far-flung bombing targets within reach. Combat aircraft, no longer limited by fuel supplies, were able to spend more time in target areas. Air Mobility Command (AMC) manages more than 546 total aircraft inventory Stratotankers, of which the Air Force Reserve and Air National Guard fly 292 in support of the AMC mission.

# BOEING 707

The Boeing 707 is a four-engine commercial passenger jet airliner developed by Boeing in the early 1950s. Its name is most commonly pronounced as "Seven Oh Seven." Boeing delivered a total of 1,010 Boeing 707s, which dominated passenger air transport in the 1960s and remained commonplace through the 1970s. The first flight of the first production 707-120 took place on December 20, 1957, and FAA certification followed on September 18, 1958. A number of changes were incorporated into the production models from the prototype. A Krueger flap was installed along the leading edge. The height of the vertical fin was increased, and a small fin was added to the underside of the fuselage to act as a bumper during excessively nose-high take-offs. The initial standard model was the 707-120 with JT3C engines, but Qantas ordered a shorter-body version called the 707-138 and Braniff ordered the higher-thrust version with Pratt & Whitney JT4A engines, the 707-220. The final major derivative was the 707-320, which featured an extended-span wing and JT4A engines. The 707-420 was the same as the 320, but with Rolls-Royce Conway turbofan engines. British certification requirements relating to engine-out go-arounds also forced Boeing to increase the height of the tail fin on all 707 variants, as well as add a ventral fin. Pan Am was the first airline to operate the 707. The aircraft's first commercial flight was from New York to Paris on October 26, 1958, with a fuel stop in Gander, Newfoundland. American Airlines operated the first domestic 707 flight on January 25, 1959. Continental Airlines introduced its first two 707 aircraft into scheduled service three months later—the first U.S. carrier to employ the type widely in domestic service. As of August 2012, only two 707s remain in service; both are in Iran.

# MIG-21

The Mikoyan-Gurevich MiG-21, known by NATO as "Fishbed," is a supersonic jet fighter aircraft, designed by the Mikoyan-Gurevich Design Bureau in the Soviet Union. It was popularly nicknamed either the "balalaika" because of the aircraft's planform-view resemblance to the Russian stringed musical instrument of the same name or the "ołówek" by Polish pilots due to the shape of its fuselage resembling a pencil. Early versions are considered second-generation jet fighters, whereas later versions are considered to be third-generation jet fighters. Some 50 countries over four continents have flown the MiG-21, and it still serves many nations a half-century after its maiden flight. The fighter made aviation records. At least by name, it is the most-produced supersonic jet aircraft in aviation history and the most-produced combat aircraft since the Korean War, and it had the longest production run of a combat aircraft (1959 to 1985 considering all variants). A total of 10,645 aircraft were built in the USSR. They were produced in three factories: GAZ 30[N 1] (3,203 aircraft) in Moscow (also known as Znamya Truda), GAZ 21 (5,765 aircraft) in Gorky [N 2], and at GAZ 31 (1,678 aircraft) in Tbilisi. Generally, Gorky built single-seaters for the Soviet forces, Moscow built single-seaters for export, and Tbilisi manufactured the twin-seaters both for export and for the USSR, although there were exceptions. The MiG-21R and MiG-21bis for export and for the USSR were built in Gorky, 17 single-seaters (MiG-21 and MiG-21F) were built in Tbilisi, the MiG-21MF was first built in Moscow and then Gorky, and the MiG-21U was built in Moscow as well as in Tbilisi. A total of 194 MiG-21F-13s were built under licence in Czechoslovakia, and Hindustan Aeronautics Ltd. of India built 657 MiG-21FLs, MiG-21Ms, and MiG-21bis.

# X-15

The North American X-15 rocket-powered aircraft was part of the X-series of experimental aircraft, initiated with the Bell X-1, that were made for the USAF, NASA, and the USN. The X-15 set speed and altitude records in the early 1960s, reaching the edge of outer space and returning with valuable data used in aircraft and spacecraft design. It currently holds the world record for the fastest speed ever reached by a manned aircraft. During the X-15 program, 13 of the flights (by eight pilots) met the USAF spaceflight criteria by exceeding the altitude of 50 miles (80.47 kilometers or 264,000 feet), thus qualifying the pilots for astronaut status; some pilots also qualified for NASA astronaut wings. Of all the X-15 missions, two flights (by the same pilot) qualified as space flights per the international FAI definition of a spaceflight by exceeding a 100-kilometer (62.137-mile or 328,084-feet) altitude. The X-15 was based on a concept study from Walter Dornberger for the NACA for a hypersonic research aircraft. The requests for proposal were published on December 30, 1954, for the airframe and on February 4, 1955, for the rocket engine. The X-15 was built by two manufacturers: North American Aviation was contracted for the airframe in November 1955, and Reaction Motors was contracted for building the engines in 1956. The first X-15 flight was an unpowered test flight by Scott Crossfield on June 8, 1959; he also piloted the first powered flight on September 17, 1959, with his first XLR-99 flight on November 15, 1960. The two XLR-11 rocket engines for the initial X-15A model delivered 72kN (16,000 lbf) of total thrust; the main engine (installed later) was a single XLR-99 rocket engine delivering 254kN (57,000 lbf) at sea level and 311 kN (70,000 lbf) at peak altitude.

# T-38 TALON

The Northrop T-38 Talon is a two-seat, twin-engine supersonic jet trainer. It was the world's first supersonic trainer and is also the most produced. The T-38 remains in service as of 2012 in air forces throughout the world. The U.S. Air Force is the largest operator of the T-38. The U.S. Naval Test Pilot School is the principal U.S. Navy operator (other T-38s were previously used as USN aggressor aircraft until replaced by the similar Northrop F-5 Tiger II). The USAF Strategic Air Command (SAC) had T-38 Talons in service from 1978 until SAC's deactivation in 1991. These aircraft were used to enhance the career development of bomber co-pilots through the "Accelerated Copilot Enrichment Program." They were later used as proficiency aircraft for all B-52 and B-1 pilots, as well as Lockheed SR-71, U-2, Boeing KC-135, and KC-10 pilots. SAC's successors, the Air Combat Command and the Air Force Global Strike Command, continues to retain T-38s as proficiency aircraft for U-2 pilots and B-2 pilots, respectively. The Air Training Command's successor, the Air Education and Training Command (AETC), uses the T-38C to prepare pilots for aircraft such as the F-15C Eagle and F-15E Strike Eagle, as well as the F-16 Fighting Falcon, B-52 Stratofortress, B-1B Lancer, B-2 Spirit, A-10 Thunderbolt, F-22 Raptor, and F-35 Lightning II. The AETC received T-38Cs in 2001 as part of the Avionics Upgrade Program. The T-38Cs owned by the AETC have undergone propulsion modernization which replaces major engine components to enhance reliability and maintainability, and an engine inlet/injector modification to increase available take-off thrust. These upgrades and modifications, with the Pacer Classic program, should extend the service life of T-38s past 2020.

# F-5

The F-5 in the forms of the Northrop F-5A/B Freedom Fighter and the F-5E/F Tiger II were less advanced than the McDonnell Douglas F-4 Phantom II, but was significantly cheaper to procure and operate leading to widespread popularity as an export fighter to U.S. allies. Despite not being procured in volume by the United States, it was perhaps the most effective air-to-air fighter possessed by the U.S. in the 1960s and early 1970s. The generally high capability, reliability, and maintainability of the F-5 is such that hundreds have remained in service with multiple air forces into the 21st century. The design team wrapped a small and highly aerodynamic fighter around two compact and high thrust-to-weight ratio General Electric J85 engines, focusing on high performance and low cost of maintenance. Armed with twin 20 mm cannons and missiles for air-to-air combat, the aircraft was also a capable ground attack platform. The first-generation F-5A entered service in the early 1960s. During the Cold War, over 800 were produced through 1972 for U.S. allies. Northrop introduced the second-generation F-5E Tiger II in 1972. This upgrade included more powerful engines, higher fuel capacity, greater wing area, and improved leading-edge extensions for better turn rate, optional air-to-air refueling, and improved avionics including air-to-air radar. Though primarily used by American allies, it also served in U.S. military aviation as a training and aggressor aircraft. A total of 1,400 Tiger II versions were built, production came to an end in 1987. The F-5 was also developed into a dedicated reconnaissance version, the RF-5 Tigereye. The Northrop F-20 Tigershark was an advanced version of the F-5E that did not find a market. The F-5N/F variants remain in service with the U.S. Navy and U.S. Marine Corps as an adversary trainer.

# BOEING 727

The Boeing 727 is a mid-size, narrow-body, three-engine, T-tail commercial jet airliner. The first Boeing 727 flew in 1963 and for over a decade it was the most-produced commercial jet airliner in the world. When production ended in 1984, a total of 1,831 aircraft had been produced. The 727's sales record for the most jet airliners ever sold was broken in the early 1990s by its younger stablemate, the Boeing 737. The 727 was produced following the success of the Boeing 707 quad-jet airliner. Designed for short-haul routes, the 727 became a mainstay of airlines' domestic route networks. A stretched variant, the 727-200, debuted in 1967. In August 2008, there were a total of 81 Boeing 727-100 aircraft and 419 727-200 aircraft in airline service. The 727 is one of the noisiest commercial jetliners, categorized as Stage 2 by the U.S. Noise Control Act of 1972, which mandated the gradual introduction of quieter Stage 3 aircraft. The 727's JT8D jet engines use older low-bypass turbofan technology whereas Stage 3 aircraft utilize the more efficient and quieter high-bypass turbofan design. When the Stage 3 requirement was being proposed, Boeing engineers analyzed the possibility of incorporating quieter engines on the 727. They determined that the JT8D-200 engine could be used on the two side-mounted pylons, but the structural work required to fit the larger-diameter engine into the fuselage structure at the number two engine location would be too great to be justifiable. At the turn of the 21st century, the 727 was still in service with a few airline fleets. However, due to changes by the U.S. FAA and the ICAO in over-water flight requirements, most major airlines had already begun to switch to twin-engine aircraft, which are more fuel-efficient and quieter than the three-engine 727. As of December 2012, 208 Boeing 727 aircraft (all variants) remain in commercial airline, private, and government service.

# C-141 STARLIFTER

The Lockheed C-141 Starlifter is a military strategic airlifter in service with the U.S. Air Force. Introduced to replace slower piston-engined cargo planes, such as the C-124 Globemaster II, the C-141 was designed to a 1960 requirement and first flew in 1963. Production deliveries of an eventual 285 began in 1965, 284 for Military Airlift Command and 1 for NASA. The aircraft remained in service for almost 40 years until the USAF withdrew the C-141 from service on May 5, 2006, replacing the aircraft with the C-17 Globemaster III. The original Starlifter model, later designated the C-141A, could carry 138 passengers, 80 litters for wounded, or 10 standard 463L master pallets with a total of 62,700 pounds (28,900 kilograms) of cargo. To correct the perceived deficiencies of the original model and to use the C-141 to the fullest, 270 C-141As were stretched, adding needed payload volume. The new variant was designated the C-141B, and the original redesignated the C-141A. Additional "plug" sections were added before and after the wings, lengthening the fuselage by 23 feet 4 inches (7.11 meters) and allowing the carriage of 103 litters for wounded, 13 standard pallets, 205 troops, 168 paratroopers, or an equivalent increase in other loads. Also added at this time was a boom receptacle for inflight refueling. The conversion program took place between 1977 and 1982. It was estimated that, in terms of increased capacity, this stretching program was the equivalent of buying 90 new aircraft. Sixty-three aircraft have been upgraded throughout the 1990s to C-141C status, with improved avionics and navigation systems, in an effort to keep them up to date until C-17s are available to replace them.

# SR-71 BLACKBIRD

The Lockheed SR-71, unofficially known as the "Blackbird" and by its crews as the "Habu," was an advanced, long-range, Mach 3 strategic reconnaissance aircraft developed from the Lockheed YF-12A and A-12 aircraft by the Lockheed Skunk Works (also responsible for the U-2 and many other advanced aircraft). It flew from 1964 to 1998. The legendary "Kelly" Johnson was the man behind many of the design's advanced concepts. The SR-71 was one of the first aircraft to have an extremely low radar signature. The aircraft flew so fast and so high that if the pilot detected a surface-to-air missile launch, the standard evasive action was simply to accelerate. No SR-71 was ever shot down. The SR-71's Pratt & Whitney J58 engines never exceeded testbench values above Mach 3.6 in unclassified tests. Given the history of the plane, the advanced and classified nature of much of its original design, and most importantly, the simple fact that no SR-71 exists in a form that is immediately airworthy, it may never be known what the true design tolerances of the aircraft were, or if these tolerances were ever approached in flight. This unverifiability undoubtedly contributes to the myths and fallacies surrounding the SR-71. The SR-71 was the first operational aircraft designed around a stealthy shape and materials. The most visible marks of its low radar cross section (RCS) are its inwardly canted vertical stabilizers and the fuselage chines. Comparably, a plane of the SR-71's size should generate a radar image the size of a flying barn, but its actual return is more like that of a single door. Though with a much smaller RCS than expected for a plane of its size, it was still easily detected because the exhaust stream would return its own radar signature.

# F-111

The General Dynamics F-111 is a long-range strategic bomber, reconnaissance, and tactical strike aircraft. The F-111's beginnings were in the TFX, an ambitious early 1960s project to combine the U.S. Air Force requirement for a fighter-bomber with the U.S. Navy's need for a long-range carrier defense fighter to replace the F-4 Phantom II and the F-8 Crusader. The fighter design philosophy of the day concentrated on very high speed, raw power, and air-to-air missiles. In June 1960 the USAF issued a specification for a long-range interdiction/strike aircraft able to penetrate Soviet air defenses at very low altitudes and very high speeds to deliver tactical nuclear weapons against crucial Soviet targets such as airfields and supply depots. The first flight of the F-111A, as the USAF version was designated, was December 21, 1964, and entry into service with the USAF began July 18, 1967. The Navy version, the F-111B (visually distinguishable from all other variants due to its noticeably shorter nose), was canceled in December 1968 to be replaced by the F-14 Tomcat, but other F-111 variants went on to serve with the USAF through the mid-1990s, performing with distinction in the 1991 Gulf War. Currently the Royal Australian Air Force is the only operator of the F-111 and continues to upgrade the aircraft with modern avionics as well as modern weapon systems.

# BOEING 737

The Boeing 737 is a short- to medium-range twin-engined narrow-bodied jet airliner. Originally developed as a shorter, lower-cost, twin-engine airliner derived from Boeing's 707 and 727, the 737 has developed into a family of nine passenger models with a capacity of 85 to 215 passengers. The 737 is Boeing's only narrow-bodied airliner in production, with the -600, -700, -800, and -900ER variants currently being built. A re-engined and redesigned version, the 737 MAX, is set to debut in 2017. It entered airline service in February 1968. The lengthened 737-200 entered service in April 1968. In the 1980s Boeing launched the -300, -400, and -500 models, subsequently referred to as the Boeing 737 Classic series. The 737 Classics added capacity and incorporated CFM56 turbofan engines along with wing improvements. In the 1990s Boeing introduced the 737 Next Generation with multiple changes, including a redesigned wing, upgraded cockpit, and new interior. The 737 Next Generation comprises the four -600, -700, -800, and -900ER models, ranging from 102 feet (31.09 meters) to 138 feet (42.06 meters) in length. Boeing also has Business Jet versions of the 737 Next Generation. The 737 series is the best-selling jet airliner in the history of aviation. The 737 has been continually manufactured by Boeing since 1967 with 7,457 aircraft delivered and 3,044 orders yet to be filled as of January 2013. The 737 assembly is centered at the Boeing Renton Factory in Renton, Washington. Many 737s serve markets previously filled by 707, 727, 757, DC-9, and MD-80/MD-90 airliners, and the aircraft currently competes primarily with the Airbus A320 family. There are, on average, 1,250 Boeing 737s airborne at any given time, with two departing or landing somewhere every five seconds.

# CONCORDE

The Aérospatiale-BAC Concorde aircraft was a turbojet-powered supersonic passenger airliner, a supersonic transport (SST). It was a product of an Anglo-French government treaty, combining the manufacturing efforts of Aérospatiale and the British Aircraft Corporation. First flown in 1969, Concorde entered service in 1976 and continued for 27 years. Concorde flew regular transatlantic flights from London Heathrow (British Airways) and Paris-Charles de Gaulle Airport (Air France) to New York JFK and Washington Dulles, profitably flying these routes at record speeds, in less than half the time of other airliners. Indeed, Concorde held many speed records. With only 20 aircraft built, the costly development phase represented a substantial economic loss. Additionally, Air France and British Airways were subsidized by their governments to buy the aircraft. As a result of the plane's only crash (on July 25, 2000), world economic effects arising from the 9/11 attacks, and other factors, operations ceased on October 24, 2003. The last "retirement" flight occurred on November 26, 2003. Concorde was an ogival (also "ogee") delta-winged aircraft with four Olympus engines based on those originally developed for the Avro Vulcan strategic bomber. The engines were jointly built by Rolls-Royce and SNECMA. Concorde was the first civil airliner to have an analogue fly-by-wire flight control system. It also employed a trademark droop snoot lowering nose section for visibility on approach. These and other features permitted Concorde to have an average cruise speed of Mach 2.02 (about 2,140 km/h or 1,330 mph) with a maximum cruise altitude of 60,000 feet (18,300 meters), more than twice the speed of conventional aircraft. The average landing speed was 298 km/h (185 mph, 160 knots).

# TUPOLEV TU-144

The Tupolev Tu-144, known by NATO as the "Charger," was the world's first supersonic transport aircraft with its first flight preceding that of Concorde. It was constructed under the direction of the Soviet Tupolev design bureau headed by Alexei Tupolev. A prototype first flew on December 3, 1968, near Moscow, two months before the first flight of the similar Aérospatiale/British Aircraft Corporation Concorde. The Tu-144 first broke the speed of sound on June 5, 1969, and on July 15, 1969, it became the first commercial transport to exceed Mach 2, and it was at the time the fastest commercial-type airliner. The Tu-144 was Tupolev's only supersonic commercial airliner venture. Tupolev's other large supersonic aircraft were designed and built to military specifications. All these aircraft benefited from technical and scientific input from TsAGI, the Central Aerohydrodynamic Institute. At the Paris Air Show on June 3, 1973, the development program of the Tu-144 suffered severely when the first Tu-144S production airliner crashed. While in the air, the Tu-144 underwent a violent downward maneuver. Trying to pull out of the subsequent dive, the Tu-144 broke up and crashed, destroying 15 houses and killing all six people on board the Tu-144 and eight more on the ground. The causes of this incident remain controversial to this day. A popular theory was that the Tu-144 was forced to avoid a French Mirage chase plane that was attempting to photograph its canards, which were very advanced for the time, and that the French and Soviet governments colluded with each other to cover up such details.

# BOEING 747

The Boeing 747, aka the "Jumbo Jet," is among the world's most recognizable aircraft and was the first wide-bodied commercial airliner ever produced. First flown commercially in 1970, it held the passenger capacity record for 37 years until it was surpassed by the Airbus A380. The four-engine 747 uses a double-deck configuration for part of its length. It is available in passenger, freighter, and other versions. Boeing designed the 747's hump-like upper deck to serve as a first-class lounge or (as is the general rule today) extra seating, and to allow the aircraft to be easily converted to a cargo carrier by removing seats and installing a front cargo door. By September 2012, 1,448 aircraft had been built, with 81 of the 747-8 variants remaining on order. The 747-400, the latest version in service, is among the fastest airliners in service with a high-subsonic cruise speed of Mach 0.85 (567 mph or 913 km/h). It has an intercontinental range of 7,260 nautical miles (8,350 miles or 13,450 kilometers). The 747-400 passenger version can accommodate 416 passengers in a typical three-class layout or 524 passengers in a typical two-class layout. The newest version of the aircraft, the 747-8, is in production and received certification in 2011. Deliveries of the 747-8F freighter version to launch customer Cargolux began in October 2011. Deliveries of the 747-8I passenger version to Lufthansa began in May 2012. The 747 is to be replaced by the Boeing Y3 (part of the Boeing Yellowstone Project) in the future.

# C-5 GALAXY

The Lockheed C-5 Galaxy is one of the largest military aircraft in the world. The C-5 is used throughout the world exclusively by the U.S. Air Force. The C-5, with its tremendous payload capability, provides the Air Mobility Command (AMC) intertheater airlift in support of United States national defense. The C-5 and the C-17 Globemaster III are partners in AMC's strategic airlift concept. The aircraft carry fully equipped combat-ready military units (including main battle tanks) to any point in the world on short notice, then provide field support required to help sustain the fighting force. On June 30, 1968, Lockheed-Georgia Co. began flight testing its new Galaxy C-5A heavy transport with the aircraft's first flight taking to the air under the call-sign "Allen-zero-three-heavy." Lockheed delivered the first operational Galaxy to the 437th Airlift Wing, Charleston Air Force Base, South Carolina, in June 1970. C-5s are stationed at Altus AFB, Oklahoma; Dover AFB, Delaware; and Travis AFB, California. AMC transferred some C-5s to the Air Reserve components starting with Kelly AFB, Texas, in 1985; followed by Stewart Air National Guard Base, New York; and Westover Air Reserve Base, Massachusetts. Beginning in October 2005 a squadron was formed at Wright-Patterson Air Force Base near Dayton, Ohio. This unit is primarily composed of aircraft transferred from Dover AFB and replaces the squadron's C-141s, which were the last C-141s to be retired. In the mid-1970s, wing cracks were found throughout the fleet. Consequently, all C-5A aircraft were restricted to a maximum of 50,000 pounds (22,700 kilograms) of cargo each. To increase their lifting capability and service life, 77 C-5As underwent a re-winging program from 1981 to 1987.

# CHENGDU J-7

The Chengdu Jian-7, known as the J-7 in China and the F-7 in export versions, is a People's Republic of China license-built version of the Soviet Mikoyan-Gurevich MiG-21. Although production ceased in 2008, it continues to serve, mostly as an interceptor, in several air forces, including China's. The Sino-Soviet split abruptly ended Chinese early participation in the developmental program of the MiG-21, and from July 28 to September 1, 1960, when the Soviet Union withdrew its advisers from China. Nikita Khrushchev reversed that decision in February 1962 when he wrote to inform Mao Zedong that the Soviet Union was ready to transfer MiG-21 technology to China and asked the Chinese to send their representatives to the Soviet Union as soon as possible to discuss the details. Russian sources stated that complete examples of the MiG-21 were flown to China by Soviet pilots, and China received MiG-21Fs in kits along with parts and technical documents. In March 1964, Shenyang Aircraft Factory began the first domestic production of the jet fighter, successfully completing the planes the next year, although full-scale production did not come about until the 1980s, by which time the design was showing its age. The J-7 only reached Soviet-designed capacity in the mid-1980s. The fighter is affordable and widely exported as the F-7, often with Western systems incorporated, such as the ones sold to Pakistan. Based on the expertise gained by this program, China later developed the Shenyang J-8 by utilizing the incomplete technical information of the Soviet Ye-152 developmental jet.

# EA-6B PROWLER

The EA-6B Prowler is a twin-engine, mid-wing aircraft manufactured by Northrop Grumman Aerospace Corporation as a modification of the basic A-6 Intruder airframe. Designed for carrier and advanced base operations, the Prowler is a fully integrated electronic warfare system combining long-range, all-weather capabilities with advanced electronic countermeasures. A forward equipment bay and pod-shaped faring on the vertical fin house the additional avionics equipment. It is the U.S. Navy's and the U.S. Marine Corps' primary electronic warfare aircraft. The primary mission of the aircraft is to support strike aircraft and ground troops by interrupting enemy electronic activity and obtaining tactical electronic intelligence within a combat area. Since the retirement of the EF-111 Raven in 1995, it is the only aerial radar jammer in the DOD arsenal. It has been utilized in practically every U.S. combat operation and is frequently loaned to the U.S. Air Force. The increased usage has shorted the airframes' lifetimes and they are slated to be replaced by the EA-18G Growler. The Prowler has a crew of four, a pilot and three electronic counter-measures officers. Powered by two non-afterburning Pratt & Whitney J52-P408 turbojet engines, it is capable of speeds of up to 950 km/h with a range of 1,840 kilometers. The Prowler is a high-maintenance aircraft and undergoes more frequent equipment upgrades than any other aircraft in the Navy. Although designed as an electronic escort and command-and-control platform for strike missions, the EA-6B is also capable of attacking surface targets—especially radars, SAM launchers, and other enemy defenses—on its own. The AGM-88 HARM (high-speed anti-radiation missile) is the main offensive strike weapon of the Prowler.

# A-10 THUNDERBOLT II

The A-10 was developed in response to the increasing vulnerability of ground-attack planes as evidenced by the large number that were shot down due to small-arms fire, surface-to-air missiles, and low-level anti-aircraft gunfire during the Vietnam War. This led to a need for a specialized, heavily armed, heavily armored aircraft. On March 6, 1967, the U.S. Air Force released a request to create a design study for a low-cost attack aircraft designated A-X, short for Attack Experimental. In May 1970, the USAF issued a modified yet much more detailed request for proposal. Six companies submitted contestants to the USAF. Northrop and Fairchild Republic were selected to build prototypes: the YA-9A and YA-10A, respectively. The first flight of the A-10 was in May 1972. After trials and a fly-off against the A-9, the USAF selected Fairchild-Republic's A-10 as the winner on January 10, 1973. The first-production A-10 flew in October 1975 and deliveries to the USAF commenced in March 1976 with 715 aircraft being produced. Production ended in 1984. The A-10/OA-10 has excellent maneuverability at low speeds and altitude thanks to wide, straight wings. These also allow short take-offs and landings, permitting operations from airfields near front lines. The plane can loiter for extended periods of time and operate under 1,000-foot (300-meter) ceilings with 1.5-mile (2.4-kilometer) visibility. It can fly at a relatively slow speed of 200 mph (320 km/h), which makes it better at ground attack than fast fighter-bombers. The "Warthog" is exceptionally hardy, with a strong airframe that can survive direct hits from armor-piercing and high-explosive projectiles. The aircraft has triple redundancy in its flight systems, with mechanical systems to back up double-redundant hydraulic systems. The aircraft is designed to fly with one engine and a wing torn off.

# JAGUAR

The SEPECAT Jaguar is an Anglo-French ground-attack aircraft in service with the Royal Air Force and several export customers, notably the Indian Air Force. The aircraft served as one of the French Air Force's main strike aircraft until July 1, 2005, when it was replaced by the Dassault Rafale. It was the product of the world's first bi-national military aircraft program. The Jaguar program began in the early 1960s in response to a British requirement for an advanced supersonic jet trainer, and a French need for a cheap, subsonic dual-role trainer and attack aircraft with good short-field performance. From these apparently disparate aims would come a single and entirely different aircraft: relatively high-tech, supersonic, and optimized for ground attack in a high-threat environment. It was planned as a replacement for the RAF Hawker Hunter and the Armee de l'Air F-100 Super Sabre. Cross-channel negotiations led to the formation of SEPECAT (the Société Européenne de Production de l'Avion d'Ecole de Combat et d'Appui Tactique) in 1966 as a joint venture between Bréguet (the design leader) and the British Aircraft Corporation to produce the airframe, and a separate teaming of Rolls-Royce and Turboméca to develop the Adour afterburning turbofan engine. The first of eight prototypes flew on September 8, 1968. It was an orthodox single-seat, swept-wing, twin-engine design but with tall landing gear. It had a maximum take-off weight in the 15-ton class and could manage a combat radius on internal fuel alone of 850 kilometers. Maximum speed was Mach 1.6 (Mach 1.1 at sea level) and hardpoints were fitted for an external weapons load of up to 10,000 pounds.

# S-3 VIKING

The Lockheed S-3 Viking is a jet aircraft used by the U.S. Navy to hunt and destroy enemy submarines and provide surveillance of surface shipping. A carrier-based, subsonic, all-weather, multi-mission aircraft with long range, it operates primarily with carrier battle groups in anti-submarine warfare roles. It carries automated weapon systems and is capable of extended missions with in-flight refueling. Because of the engines' high-pitched sound, the plane is nicknamed the "Hoover" after the brand of vacuum cleaner. The S-3 is a conventional monoplane with a high-mounted cantilever wing, swept 15 degrees. It is powered by two turbofan engines mounted in nacelles under the wings. The aircraft can seat four crew members with the pilot and the copilot/tactical coordinator in the front of the cockpit and the tactical coordinator and sensor operator in the back. All crew members sit on upward-firing zero-zero ejector seats. The wing is fitted with leading edge and Fowler flaps. Spoilers are fitted to both the upper and lower surfaces of the wings. All control surfaces are actuated by dual hydraulically boosted irreversible systems. The aircraft has two underwing hardpoints that can be used to carry fuel tanks, general purpose and cluster bombs, missiles, rockets, and storage pods. It also has four internal bomb bay stations that can be used to carry general purpose bombs and torpedoes. A number of sonobuoy chutes are fitted, and there are three dispensers for chaff, flares, and expendable jammers. A retractable magnetic anomaly detector boom is fitted in the tail.

# F-14 TOMCAT

The Grumman F-14 Tomcat was a U.S. Navy supersonic, twin-engine, swing-wing, two-seat interceptor. The Tomcat's primary missions were air superiority and fleet air defense, although it later acquired the ability to strike ground targets with precision munitions. It entered service in 1972 with the U.S. Navy, replacing the F-4 Phantom II. It was later exported to the Imperial Iranian Air Force in 1976. It was retired from the U.S. Navy in September 2006 and replaced by the F/A-18E/F Super Hornet, although it remains in service with the Islamic Republic of Iran Air Force. The Tomcat consists of a high forward nacelle containing the radar and cockpits and two widely spaced engines arranged around a flat fuselage that contains the variable geometry mechanism. The fuselage alone forms over half of the aircraft's lifting surface. The space between the engines allows for carriage of many external stores in a less aerodynamically intrusive manner than on the wings, in a manner remniscent of the A-5 Vigilante. The variable geometry wings would have required complex pylons to remain aligned with the airstream, as on the F-111B. The F-14 has an additional pair of hardpoints on the fixed vane portion of the wing. In the 1990s, with the pending retirement of the A-6 Intruder, the F-14 air-to-ground program was resurrected. Trials with live bombs were carried out in the 1980s, and the F-14 was cleared to use basic iron bombs in 1992. In Operation Desert Storm, most air-to-ground missions were left to A-7 and F/A-18 squadrons, with the F-14 focusing on air defense operations. Following Desert Storm, F-14As and F-14Bs underwent upgrades to avionics and cockpit displays to enable the use of precision munitions, enhance defensive systems, and apply structural improvements.

# F-15 EAGLE

The Boeing (formerly McDonnell Douglas) F-15 Eagle is an American-built all-weather tactical fighter designed to gain and maintain air superiority in aerial combat. It first flew in July 1972. A derivative of the aircraft is the F-15E Strike Eagle, a highly successful all-weather strike fighter which entered service in 1988. The F-15's maneuverability is derived from low wing loading (weight to wing area ratio) with a high thrust-to-weight ratio enabling the aircraft to turn tightly without losing airspeed. The F-15 can climb to 30,000 feet in around 60 seconds. The F-15's versatile APG-63/70 pulse-doppler radar system can look up at high-flying targets and down at low-flying targets without being confused by ground clutter. It can detect and track aircraft and small high-speed targets at distances beyond visual range down to close range and at altitudes down to tree-top level. The radar feeds target information into the central computer for effective weapons delivery. For close-in dogfights, the radar automatically acquires enemy aircraft and this information is projected on the head-up display. The F-15's electronic warfare system provides both threat warning and automatic countermeasures against selected threats. When the pilot changes from one weapon system to another, visual guidance for the required weapon automatically appears on the head-up display. The F-15E Strike Eagle is a two-seat, dual-role, totally integrated fighter for all-weather, air-to-air, and deep interdiction missions. The rear cockpit is upgraded to include four multi-purpose CRT displays for aircraft systems and weapons management. The digital, triple-redundant Lear Siegler flight control system permits coupled automatic terrain following, enhanced by a ring-laser gyro inertial navigation system.